SONG LEAVES.

SONG LEAVES

FROM THE

BOOK OF LIFE AND NATURE.

BY AN AMERICAN.

> Oh deem not, midst this worldly strife,
> An idle art the Poet brings:
> Let high Philosophy control,
> And sages calm the stream of life,
> 'Tis he refines its fountain-springs,
> The nobler passions of the soul.
> — CAMPBELL.

NEW YORK:
J. S. REDFIELD, CLINTON HALL.
1852.

ENTERED according to Act of Congress in the year One Thousand Eight Hundred and Fifty-Two,

BY M. B. WYNKOOP,

In the Clerk's Office of the District Court of the United States, for the Southern District of New York.

PREFACE.

Though Poetry may be classed among the elegancies of Literature, and be looked upon more as an ornamental appendage to the library and drawing-room than as a source of amusement or instruction, it has its mission upon earth as well as writings in prose. And that mission is to speak unto the hearts of men. To place itself on the side of Virtue and Truth; and, by its pictures of Life and Nature, graced, as the artist may be able, with the drapery of Romance, or the colors of Fancy, draw mankind closer together in bonds of sympathy and fellowship. And, while cultivating a taste for the Beautiful in Art and Nature, raise in the breast a desire to extend those earthly blessings which Providence has showered upon them to their less fortunate brethren.

There have been occasions when a simple song has effected more than volumes of prose. Hood's "Song of the Shirt" is a memorable instance of the influence of Poetry; for it tended more to the amelioration of an unfortunate class of English laborers than the

PREFACE.

efforts of humane societies for years. In ancient times the influence of song was more regarded than at present. The wandering minstrel seemed to possess a magic power in his harp and rudely-chaunted song; for he roused warriors to heroic deeds, and drew tears from the eyes of women. He was placed at the head of armies to inspirit the soldiers, and when Peace smiled, no festive board was complete without the presence of a bard. Yet, even in late years, there have been poets whose power over the hearts of men is indeed marvellous. The songs of BURNS are as familiar as household words, not only in Scotland, but the world over, from India to the far West; and the Scotchman feels his blood tingling in his veins at the martial strains of "Scots wha hae," or melts into tears when he listens to the touching farewell to "Highland Mary."

In this utilitarian age, however, he who would inculcate great truths had better, probably, write in prose; for poetry, in weak hands, is a powerless weapon. It is only the masters of Poesy who can command not only the ears, but the hearts of men. This should have been sufficient, it may be said, to have warned me from a field where the chances of success are more than counterbalanced by the probabilities of failure. To this I can offer but a weak excuse. Conscious of my own unworthiness, yet proud of being even a humble laborer in the cause of philanthropy and human progress, my enthusiasm may have led me beyond the bounds of prudence, and caused me to undertake that which was far above my abilities; yet the purity of my motives will sustain

...e, and I will have a nobler satisfaction in failing in a praiseworthy ...fort, than had I succeeded in an ignoble one.

These "Song Leaves" are but fragments, and, it must be con-...ssed, thrown together with little order or sequence. Parts in ...emselves may be considered complete, so far as I was capable; ...ut as a whole, I would indeed be blind not to see that it is a very ...sufficient poem. This is a source of regret to me: not that my ...anity led me to suppose I had the genius necessary for the pro-...uction of a finished work, but that I have fallen so far below even ...y own conceptions, and that which I pictured in my mind, my ...oor abilities as a writer failed to do justice to in language. But ...frankly own that I have done my best, be it for better or worse, ...nd as such submit my Leaves to the public, not without misgiv-...gs, yet hoping the reader may at least be as kind as I have been ...andid.

THE AUTHOR.

NEW YORK, January, 1852.

SONG LEAVES.

I.

Could I but sing as sang our bards of yore—
Could I but strike the much-loved, honored lyre—
Revive the notes the world may hear no more—
The Nine I might invoke my theme t' inspire,
And tune with conscious hand the golden wire:
But now the strains of song are growing mute,
And dust remaining of the classic fire:—
 At such a time, this humble lay may suit—
This unpretending tale, chimed to a broken lute.

II.

To paint the varied scenes of mortal life,
To show the passions of the human breast;
The homely quiet, and the busy strife,
Scenes of despair, and visions of the blest;
Of Nature's view the worst—the loveliest,—
These are the themes which fill my humble lay,
With no profusion of the graces dressed.
A song of life—man's little holiday—
Bedecked perchance with flowers, for Life is but a May.

III.

No vaunted theme, as poets sometimes boast,
Nor matchless story—nor a flight sublime—
No midnight revel, woman's name to toast—
Nor rapt narration of a bloody crime;
Nor yet to laud the frailties of my time;
I strike my harp to nobler songs than these:
To honest fame my aspirations climb,
If won by truth—by no attempts to please:—
Such fame, alas! on earth, true virtue seldom sees!

IV.

Turn to the mazy labyrinth of man,
If but a moment to your calling true,
And ponder long on Heaven's mystic plan.
Survey the scene in each, in every hue,
Explore the mirror with expanded view:
Rise with the thought, and startle with the scene,
And freely grasp what reason renders you,
As Nature rudely runs or moves serene:
For he who would be learned must search with senses keen.

V.

Wouldst Nature read? Then trace the growing mind,
With intuitious step, though pace sublime,
Through all the movements of its changing kind.
Trace from the infant up to manhood's prime;
Each virtue note, and even mark the crime.
These from one head alike in Nature came,
And, save th' impression stamped by diff'rent clime,
To man's imperfect sense were all the same,
And all as infants seemed consigned to mutual fame.

VI.

Then to the grave continued search pursue,
Winding thy way through Life's incessant jars.
How many differ, and agree how few!
There sleeps the hero of a hundred wars,
Filled with his glory, covered with his scars;
One a peasant lived, and a peasant died;
This one was killed by unpropitious stars;
One moved the phantom of a fashioned pride;
Here lies affection's son, and there the parricide.

VII.

One died an idiot;—another, great
In what the stars 'tis said most men refuse,
Is called the noblest genius of the state;
One born an heir to wealth he could not use,
Except his conscience and his health t' abuse;
This one a life in dusty garrets led,
A devotee to morals and the muse;—
A crust his dinner, and a straw his bed,
Though now a monument towers proudly o'er his head.

VIII.

The poorest the richest is in future fame,
Despite the incongruity of birth.
The wealthy sot, who cares to hear his name;
One from his loft with morals blessed the earth;
The rich unheeding passed the widow's hearth;
His gold he squandered, or in piles it lay;
No penny grant to aid impov'rished worth;
He would not wipe the orphan's tears away,
But seemed delighted with the miseries of his day.

IX.

But all were infants from one mother's breast.
With kindly care has Nature all begot,
And at their birth of equal parts possessed;
Yet life impulsive caused each diff'rent lot,
Alike the palace and the simple cot.
All men in nature own a kindred aim.
Alas! for him who has this truth forgot—
On each depends the structure of his fame,
To be revered as great, or doomed to lasting shame.

X.

Oh! curse not Heaven, fool, in paltry rage,
E'en though at first thou canst not rightly see,
Nor with thy just reward a warfare wage;
Contented rest, whate'er thy lot may be,
Thy fame, thy fortune, alike depend on thee.
Ne'er rise like bubbles from a cauldron's boil
The men whose station is futurity.
The fates are kind, and if thyself wilt toil,
The wondrous earth to thee displays her richest spoil.

XI.

Doth fame arise to be the feast of fools,
Helping to morsels sweet a craven mass,
Bound by the stigma of their slavish rules?
Lives in a dress of silk, or sounds in brass—
Reflects its visage in delusion's glass—
Resting where it can, praising as it goes,
That adulation may its praise surpass;
Sports on each breath of air that lightly blows,
As frail as fleeting as the winter's latest snows?

XII.

Avaunt! such foul and desecrating fame,
And at its very birth in fetters die.
Fair Honor shrinks from such a spotted shame.
Oh! bright Fame's temple shines in groves on high,
Shedding its golden lustre o'er the sky!
A world is toiling at its mountain base;
Yet few can dare, but those of eagle eye
And iron soul, to meet its dazzling face:
—Around the structure crawl with snail, but eager pace.

XIII.

Thus the spirit dreams. Turn ye to the sage,
Whose days have numbered three-score years and ten,
And wisdom learn from gray experienced age.
These flights to him are childhood's folly. When
Laboring in the world 'mong busy men
His passions were as ours; but now he feels
His soul rise o'er this futile strife: again
The glitt'ring robe of Youth his fancy steals,
While Memory thro' the breast rings her discordant peals.

XIV.

There is a reck'ning of his every deed
Which constitutes his pleasure or his pain,
Whether 'tis virtuous prize, or sinful meed.
A spotless conscience, free from cankered stain,
Devoid of dreaming Horror's fatal bane,
Is dearer far than trumpeted applause.
If he be not accursed, like branded Cain,
He loves o'er former scenes, with pensive pause,
To muse, think what will be, then smile upon what was.

XV.

Such worldly fame. Oh! nobler far than this,
(Whose sweets comprise what mankind here may know)
To taste in yonder spheres immortal bliss!
Better far than a thousand wreaths below
To feel the smile of Heaven's eternal glow.
Ah! there no sorrows pang, no pleasures cloy;
But from that fountain peaceful blessings flow.
Oh! what were man debarred from future joy—
What crimes, what follies, would this mortal life employ!

XVI.

View the aspiring youth, whose every aim
And act of life, as if for naught else sent,
Tends to one point, the winning of a name.
His every thought, his every labor bent,
Impulsed by passion and by fierce intent,
On one fond hope, to bud, to bloom, to fade—
An hour to glitter,—then its goss'mere rent,
Like the short passion of deceptive maid;
And what must wither joy's delusively delayed.

XVII.

Health, Peace, and Happiness, are cast aside;
These are as naught; for pain is sweeter yet,
When Fancy flutters in her wildest pride.
It seemed as if his all in one focus met—
The orb of Genius there had early set
Its humid glow, its wild, revolving sphere:
His source of song to be some fond regret,
Swayed by a sea of thought, perchance a tear;
For such has often forced mankind to tasks severe.

XVIII.

The cloud has burst—the glitt'ring dream is o'er—
Life's noon is hast'ning on; its morn has passed.
What his hopes have been, they can be no more;
For he in other scenes is rudely cast,
And finds his fatal error out at last.
If he be wise, his joys may yet increase.
Enough of woes has he in youth amassed.
—Devotes his future days to placid peace,
And thus no longer owns the follies of caprice.

XIX.

Perchance he turns misanthrope—hates mankind—
Alike the vile and virtuous.   Broods on care.
No kindly heart can his cold feeling find:
No beauteous spirit 'mong earth's winsome fair,
He reckons as his own.   The fickle air
More steadfast deems he than a woman.   He
Looks at the world through contortion's glass, bare
And barren as his own philosophy.
Observes no beaming lights that gild mortality.

XX.

" Go breathe your tales of love to other ears :
  'Tis not for me to heed the flatt'ring strain,
  Nor tremble at the lover's burning tears;
  Nor feel the rapture of the dreamy pain.
  Ah ! once I loved ; but let it go. 'Tis vain
  To rake anew the ashes of the past.
  I know those scenes can never be again,—
  The latest recollection's flitting fast;
But thoughts shall always burn—the tomb receive the last.

XXI.

" Oh ! could I feel as I once felt of yore,
  Ere Love's romance was dimmed by riper years !
  My dreamy hours those faded scenes deplore,
  Although the retrospection starts no tears ;
  But every thought my longing more endears."
  That man will love his woes is passing strange ;
  But when they're unalloyed by guilty fears,
  He treasures them as sweet. All Fancy's range
Yield not the pleasing thrills that thro' his bosom change.

XXII.

" 'Tis madness thus to mourn, and yet 'tis sweet,
When o'er that fatal Past my mem'ries steal,
The Present's aching pains on pinions fleet
Glide swiftly by. My aching senses reel
With new-born joy; but Life's discordant peal
Dissolves the spell. A moment thus: 'tis gone,
And I am left to pangs I scarce can feel;
For 'neath such weight of woes I grow like stone,
Unloved—nor love the world—and happiest when alone."

XXIII.

Well, let him hate. He thinks it is his joy,
Yet 'tis his heart's poison. His soul's distress
Is measured by his curses: they destroy
The *hope*, nor quench the *thirst* for tenderness.
Leave the soul blighted, yet leave him tearless.
Much is he anguished, while he smiles disgust
On earth and all its scenes of happiness.
Perchance he curses Heaven; says we're thrust
Upon the world to bear the frailties of our dust.

XXIV.

What anchoret ere sought the forest wild
From love of solitude ? 'Tis true that thrills
Of ecstacy the bosom swell, when piled
Around are Nature's heights, meand'ring rills
Licking their mossy feet. With rapture fills
The breast of him who views fair Sylvia's scene.
Her amphitheatre of rolling hills ;
Her spreading vales, with grassy velvet green ;
Her spirit visible in Summer's smiles serene.

XXV.

A woodland ramble in the month of May,
When blushing Spring in queenly car has rolled,
And Nature's bloom is beautifully gay,
Almost too lovely for an earthly mould,
Is joy to a feeling man. To behold
The op'ning flowers spreading their many dyes
Of crimson, azure, or of yellow gold,
Blessed by the nurt'ring smile of Heaven's skies,
Delights the sense of him who is not vainly wise.

XXVI.

He that admires these beauties most, would cloy
With constant gaze ; and what at first was fair
To view, less worthy than an infant's toy
Would he esteem, if his perpetual care
Should be expatiation's fruit to bear !
The tortured victim in his dungeon chained,
Breathing his last 'mid foul pollution's air,
Dies in a heaven to him, whose life is stained
With dark misanthropy—whose every pleasure 's feigned.

XXVII.

Happier than him is the galley slave,
Condemned for life to labor at the oar ;
Himself in fetters, while the buoyant wave
Dashes its unchained waters on the shore,
Thund'ring its freedom in its breakers' roar.
Perchance a wife for him doth sadly grieve ;
He sighs that he can never see her more.
Ah, this is misery ; but canst believe
This victim ever shares the misanthrope's sleepless eve ?

XXVIII.

Who has not sighed for some secluded spot,
Some peaceful nook, beyond the world's turmoil,
To live with her he loved in simple cot,
Where Love would rule, and gentle Virtue's smile
Would all the longings of the heart beguile?
In this contented scene man's woes might rest,
Forgetful of his daily work the while,
And solace find on kindling Beauty's breast,—
Live here in peace, and be on earth supremely blest.

XXIX.

A sylvan home within a quiet dell—
Could man's romantic bliss aspire to more?
No hermit's grot, but Love's enraptured cell!
The woodbine hangs around the cottage door,
The velvet moss arrays the outward floor;
An arbor festooned with the choicest flowers,
Wreathed with the circling jasmine rambling o'er,
Scenteth with fragrant air the summer hours,
And glitters in the morn with the dew's silvery showers.

XXX.

The lover busied with each homely task,
(For labor's sweat doth wash dull care away,)
To please his love is all his heart would ask;
Now tills the ground, now weaves the garland gay,
To gem her brow, the sweetest Queen of May!
And she with smiles rewards each little care;
And these, as sportive o'er her cheek they stray,
To him enough of fond love's mutual share,
With nectared kiss from lips luxuriously fair.

XXXI.

In spring they rise when rings the matin song,
Swelling with the odors of early dawn,
In soft vibration, or in cadence long,
Of blue-bird, robin, in each varied tone,
Uncouth the music, but 'tis Nature's own.
Forth from their trellissed home they take their way,
Their nostrils feasted with the flowers, new-blown,
And simple tasks begin the busy day,
Which ends not till the sun sheds his declining ray.

XXXII.

Changed is the scene when Winter's boist'rous breath,
Madly rioting in its wildest mirth,
Nips the frail bud, and hastes the flowerets' death.
When curtained night has veiled the frozen earth,
The two are seated by the blazing hearth:
Bright glows the fire, but love is brighter yet;
For there Life's fondest thrills have welcome birth.
The blaze that Virtue feeds can never set,
Nor Sorrow's tears may quench, tho' eyes be always wet!

XXXIII.

They kiss the jocund face of infancy;
The dearest blessing of their happy fate!
Ah! blissful lot! what pleasures equal thee?
The pomp of palaces, and riches' state;
Seats of the envied, stations of the great;
All the glories of a halcyon old;
The gilded flauntings that on Fashion wait;
Dross to this little spot, Contentment's fold,
Where peace is Virtue's own, and not exchanged for gold.

XXXIV.

Come to the grave! Let musing Fancy pause,
And scan mortality with searching eye,
And view the just working of Nature's laws.
Let Reason ponder, and let Mercy sigh
O'er man, that thing of dust, who lives to die:
A moment breathes, the creature of a day,
Then, like the flitting wind, sinks gaspingly.
Here nations yet unborn shall mould away,
And mingle with our dust in Oblivion's decay.

XXXV.

The grave! What troubles cease upon its brink!
Here mankind's earthly hopes must curb their flight;
And, while from their ethereal home they sink,
The dust is shrouded in eternal night!
Who can say when the Future's dawning light
Shall tear this nebulæ from the silent tomb?
That rests with Heaven. Shall bigots say what right
Have we the aid of reason to assume?   [gloom?
Or shall our thoughts expand to light Life's journey's

XXXVI.

Here let us turn with retrospective sight
O'er years and ages numbered with the dead.
What we have been, reflection may excite
To know what we may be. When life has sped,
Sensation sinks: and then the soul, 'tis said,
To this inanimate mass no longer clings,
But by a power divine through Heaven 'tis led,
And plumes itself upon angelic wings,
And then no longer owns mortality's sharp stings.

XXXVII.

Thou bigoted idolator of chance!
Canst thou stand near this grave and still deny
An immortality of soul? A glance,
Methinks, upon yon azure-spreading sky,
Filling with hundred dreams the brain, the eye,
In admiration of a higher mind
Would fix thy thoughts in deep humility.
Then view the complications of mankind!
Mortals who cannot see, to Nature's truths are blind.

XXXVIII.

Is't hard to die ?   To leave the gay, green earth,
And in one little hour from being pass ?
Does there not come o'er us a dreary dearth
At the bare thought, as in reflection's glass
We plainly see what young existence was ;
And shuddering that youth must soon grow old,
Die, perish, and fade to a rotten mass ;
That round such forms will gather the green mould,
As in the tomb they lie, so pulseless, dumb, and cold ?

XXXIX.

Nay, it is not so very hard to die !
True, 'tis a pang to part from each and all
That we have loved, and cherished long.   And why ?
Does not that death our bodies disenthrall
From hopes, fears, and everything that's mortal ?
'Tis true, 'tis vain to weep, we must concede ;
But who can look unmoved upon the pall ?
Whose breast doth not with sighing mourners bleed,
And feel that haughty man is like the frailest reed ?

XL.

On those high hills our boyhood loved to climb,—
One's native cot to look upon no more!
Those much-loved lips to kiss for the last time!
To see this as a dream that soon is o'er!
To feel we're in a barque that leaves the shore
Where all we ever cherished doth abide!
The mind still holds the hues those loved things wore,
While we are drifting on an unknown tide,
'Mid dark and gloomy clouds, alone, without a guide!

XLI.

Not so, poor soul! There is a brilliant star
Shining above thee on that boundless deep,
Which bids thee on to realms where angels are.
Then, shout with joy! It is not wise to weep
O'er blasted crops when thou mayst others reap.
Bear bravely up: thy past, thy present scan;
And look on death as a refreshing sleep;
And when the lamp of life grows pale and wan,
Die peacefully, and prove thy title still to man.

XLII.

Look on this grave. Is this the last of man?
Doth that frail board forever shroud from view
His earthly being? And doth the proud span
Of mortal hopes here lose their latest clue,
And 'scape his fellow's searching eye. 'Tis true,
This dust is food for worms; but doth remain
That which will survive decay; what man knew
But little of—his own, unsought-for gain,
His high reward for years of earthly toil and pain!—

XLIII.

Away with forms! Let inward feeling speak:
Let naught of man's frail structure curb the sway
Of Reason. What we are, and what we seek,
Should form the study of our little day.
He loses much who would in vain delay
Permit his hours to pass unheeded by.
He little recks the frailties of our clay
Who sports o'er Life's garden like a butterfly;
His days are but a dream—he wakes, alas! to die!

XLIV.

Man is but the creature of his instinct;
The mind, the inward power, that instinct sways,
And turns wheresoe'er it will; but there is linked
With us that which lives pervading—which stays
Its unknown course for naught; but, 'neath the blaze
Of ambitious hopes, grows to raging fire,
Blighting as 't onward rolls; its living rays
Waft in seeming glory earth's longings higher;
Then bursts the cloud, and dust alone is on the pyre!

XLV.

Such is the SOUL.   Alas! unhappy gift!
Yet, what were man without that inward power?
That God-like attribute perchance may lift
Mortality from earth.   In Fancy's hour
The soul may revel in a heavenly bower;
And, in the vision of that pictured flight,
If through the veil, where clouds of darkness lower,
The mind may search its way, what glorious light
Shows to th' astonished gaze Elysium so bright!

XLVI.

Perverted custom is alone the fault,
For Nature never bends nor swerves her course.
Superstition may sometimes wish to vault
To immortality at once: the force
Of reason is thus frozen at its source,
And man, in ignominious fetters cast,
Struggles with forbidden truths in whispers hoarse,
And pregnant souls undelivered breathe their last,
For fear the dreadful night of Ignorance has not passed.

XLVII.

Beware of cant. It is religion's bane.
And blest the man who feels a nobler thrill
Than he who bows before the holy fane
To satisfy a custom. Not His will
He then obeys, for thoughts polluted fill
His panting breast, while breathes the gaudy prayer
In mockery of words, and Fashion's tinsel,
To stamp him as a genius. Such we are:
Few bold enough to rise, and lay our blackness bare.

XLVIII.

Stop by this tomb ; 'tis of a maiden fair
Who perished in her youth. The simple tale
Was told me by an old and childless pair.
A thoughtless boy, I heard their saddened wail,
And saw the tear start forth, the cheek grow pale.
Their daughter loved, and was beloved by one
Whose ship would soon across the ocean sail :
The day was fixed ; but now he must be gone, [flown.
And would be back to her when three short moons had

XLIX.

Upon his manly breast the woman hung,
While Sorrow's briny tears flowed hot and fast,
And sobs were all the language of her tongue.
Oh ! was it true ?—Did she behold the last
Of him she loved ? Was love so quickly past ?
Gaze, woman, gaze ; for thou shalt see no more.—
The ship now rides obedient to the blast :
—Adieu ! adieu ! His boat is at the shore—
One mutual sigh and kiss.—The parting scene is o'er.

L.

A year rolled by—she heard not of his fate—
With silent sorrow wore her soul away.
Would he come now, alas! 't would be too late;
Her health and beauty all had seen their day,
And life is ebbing fast, nor brooks delay.
Fit tenant for the household of the dead,
With broken heart and blasted hopes. The clay
Of earth to be her promised nuptual bed;
And worms must fester in that passion's eye-lit head!

LI.

But why narrate? Such tales are numberless:
Unhappy love, in woman only true!
Man cannot feel that deep, that sore distress
That pales the lustre of the cheek's red hue,
Then snaps the brittle cord of life in two.
Thy love was faithful, yet thou lovedst in vain;
For he was shrouded in the ocean's blue!
But here thou restest, freed from mortal pain;
And let us fondly hope that ye have met again!

LII.

A weary trav'ller from a distant land
Had sought the village of his early days.
The summer's evening air was sweetly bland,
The moon was shining in her lambent rays:
Along the well-known path he ling'ring stays,
And wipes the gath'ring moisture from his eye:
Thus at Affection's shrine his homage pays,
While faithful Mem'ry starts the mournful sigh,
As each familiar spot the traveller passes by.

LIII.

Ah! there in childhood's hours he idly played!
Close where the greenwood meets his ravished view,
He roved by moonlight with his chosen maid;
And here, alas! she heard his sad adieu!
And muses thus:—" Ah! then I little knew
That youth and youthful hours are but a dream;
That riper age reflects a darker hue,
Robbing that era of its golden gleam;
That Fancy's airy flights are not what all they seem.

LIV.

"Fair maiden of my younger, happier days,
　Upon thy lover, weeping here below,
If such may be, with angel's sweetness gaze;
　Nor mark his tears; for, ah! the heart doth know
They are not half the type of mortal wo!
　Could but thy soul from some bright planet shine,
And shed on me its mystic, heavenly glow,
　My wreaths above thy grave I still might twine
By night, and dream I clasped thy gentle hand in mine.

LV.

"A sadd'ning silence broods upon the scene:
　Cold Melancholy flits on ebon wing
O'er what is nothing now, but which has been
　A day's beauty—a floweret of the Spring—
'Round which an hundred graces seemed to cling;
　But now, alas! they all are nothingness!
That mellow voice has ceased its tones to ring;
　The winds no more shall kiss thy raven tress;
And only Mem'ry keeps thy hues of loveliness.

LVI.

" Why should we mourn ?   Say, is it wise to shed
　Our tears upon the graves of those we love,
　The living thus lamenting for the dead,
　Who may perchance smile on us from above,
　As through those halcyon scenes their spirits rove?
　Yes, 'tis manly : affection hallows pain,
　And hard the heart that would a tear remove
　Which animates the Past.   It is not vain
To weep, and in our tears to kiss those lips again !

LVII.

" The beechen tree !   One idle, summer's day
　We carved our names upon its yielding rind.
　Still can I trace them by the moon's faint ray !
　Noble Harry !   A heart more gen'rous, kind,
　Than thine, my search on earth shall never find.
　My honest Will ! ah, would that thou wert here,
　With me to whisper to the midnight wind
　Melancholy dirges o'er Harry's bier, ·
With me to freely shed the sympathetic tear.

LVIII.

" Yes! then we wondered who these names would read
　When years had flown in Time's revolving flight;
　Whose breast o'er faded scenes should sadly bleed.
　Mine be the lot to view the frosty blight
　That came, as 't were, in one bleak, wintry night,
　To blast the summer of our youth.　To me
　It seems but yesterday, when clear and bright
　The summer's sun shone on the beechen tree,
As 'neath its ample shade we romped in boyish glee.'

LIX.

There is a moral in this humble tale:
The names thus lightly carved in boyhood's play
'Neath Time's obliterating hand shall fail
To show their faint impression.　Such the stay
Of mortal hopes, the bauble of a day.
—Man scrawls his name upon Life's sandy shore;
Time's rolling sea soon sweeps the lines away;
The traceless sand is then re-written o'er;
Again is swallowed up in Time's eternal roar.

LX.

More hallowed scenes now meet the wand'rer's view—
His youthful home—his parent's simple cot!
Each bush, each little nook, how well he knew!
The small enjoyments of their humble lot.
But, ah! how changed! Time's with'ring, blighting rot
Alike o'er high and low its canker throws.
—Yes! here the garden bloomed; but now 'tis not.
The loathsome weed usurped the fading rose,—
All, all, its slow decay too plainly, sadly shows!

LXI.

There is a mound beneath a willow tree
In the churchyard's corner. Its crumbling stone
Shows of a name the faded tracery.
He kneels upon the grass, and, one by one,
He cons the letters o'er. His task is done;
His lips press on the sod. 'Twas Heaven gave
This mournful solace to her wand'ring son,
Ere ceased the swelling of Life's fitful wave,
To weep by night upon his sainted mother's grave!

LXII.

Tread lightly o'er this earth, Alonzo lies
Beneath its stone;—'tis graven with his name.
Alas! how Death on lightning pinions flies!
He was my earliest friend, and thus became
Linked with my heart. And Friendship's holy flame
Assumed a brighter glow as years flew on.
In pain or joy, his kindness still the same:
Gentle, though proud; yet never stooped to fawn;
Why praise his noble deeds? 'Tis vain; but he is gone!

LXIII.

In Alonzo's grave is buried every strife,
If aught could envy him. But let it pass—
Hatred flees with the ending of his life.
Green be our thoughts of him as this thick grass
That still lives on through winter's snow. Alas!
Our memories will fade with coming years,
When thoughts are added in confusion's mass.
Ah! then will be erased these burning tears—
Some new perception charms—forget what now endears.

LXIV.

One Summer's eve, beside a new-made mound,
With lilies in her hand, I saw a child,
Which one by one she cast upon the ground;
Close to each stem the yellow clay she piled,
And seemed to say, "Grow! lilies, grow!" She smiled
Upon her task, and stooped to kiss the leaves
Of th' emblem of purity undefiled.
Thus childish love o'er Death a garland weaves,
While Manhood vainly weeps, and long in sadness grieves!

LXV.

"Whose grave, my child, do you thus fondle o'er?"
"My mother's, sir; this was her fav'rite flower!
They tell me I can never see her more,
And yet I always bring at ev'ning's hour
My lilies to receive the dewy shower.
At morn I come to see their sparkling white.
When they cease to bloom, from my mother's bower
I'll clip the cypress vine, whose stems so light
I'll twine me in a wreath, and cast it here at night."

LXVI.

"Your sire, my child?" "He fell at Monterey;
They said it killed her; but she shed no tear,
And told me he'd gone to Heaven. From that day
She loved me more than ever; and when a year
Had flown around, she lay upon her bier!"
Simple, guileless child! would that I like you
Could smile above the dust that I revere!
A breath of love to be my last adieu,
And yet in Memory's cell to be as fondly true!

LXVII.

Oh, War, Havoc, Rapine, and Slaughter! ye
Have made this beauteous earth a very hell!
Before your with'ring blasts Peace, Comfort flee,
And Mercy lingers o'er a sad farewell,
While Death is hastening to sound his knell.
In undistinguished mass, the old, the young,
Have fallen 'neath your scourge. Ah, who shall tell
What hearts your woes, your miseries have wrung?
To breathe but half the tale could Poesy find a tongue?

LXVIII.

Shades of the Past, invoking shades to be!
(And, oh, may man here learn to hate ye more,
Viewing the woes ye give humanity!)
—Red and bloated War, stiff with crimsoned gore,
With clank of steel, the wide field rattles o'er;
Close on the monarch's step his subjects wait,
Hell's furies breathing from their every pore—
The spirits dread that rule delusive fate,
And prove th' awful bane of many a conquered state.

LXIX.

Despair, gaunt visaged, in her weeds arrayed,
While Moloch thunders from the field afar,
And Murder startles with her bloody blade;
Black Carnage sits upon the demon's car,
O'er which the furies bear his fatal star:
Swift as the wind these monster spirits speed
To glut with blood the roaring mouth of War,
While all their own destructive passions feed,
And revel in the gore, as millions 'round them bleed.

LXX.

Exulting Fame now builds her throne on high,
And adds the nerve which youthful heroes lack,
And holds in rapturous awe each gazing eye;
But Death, from the hot field awhile held back,
Soon runs his course, and leaves a bloody track;
Before him Glory flees, and Fame withdraws,
The sky, meanwhile, in thick clouds looming black,
And Horror grim fills up the dreadful pause,
As Nature mourns alone her violated laws.

LXXI.

Avaunt the scene! For milder spirits haste
To bid this foul, unholy combat cease,
And drive Destruction from the gloomy waste.
See mild Affection, with celestial Peace,
While Virtue's smiles bid kindling joys increase;
Stern Justice, rampant o'er the meaner clay,
Balances the follies of man's caprice;
These with their countless blessings strew the way,
And heavenly choirs conclude the regenerated day.

LXXII.

See, 'tis a gala day ! Rich streamers float,
And through the sky their serpent wreathing strays :
In silver strains the sounding trumpet's throat
Swells the loud paen in the hero's praise,
While silken banners bright effulgence raise :
With thunder shouts resounds th' admiring crowd,
And thus its share of empty homage pays ;
But soon forgetful whom its zeal avowed,
It hails some diff'rent star, and spurns where once it bowed.

LXXIII.

Such is the trumpeting of vain applause.
Wouldst live forever? Then seek a nobler aim
Than pand'ring to the world. Some gen'rous cause
That feeds its own desires : that brass-tongued fame
Can never couple with a paltry name.
Go where Affliction shows the sunken eye—
To haunts of vice—to dens of sin and shame :
With fallen Virtue in contrition sigh—
Afford the needful aid when Death is hov'ring nigh.

LXXIV.

I see a village by a river's side;
The homely cots strewn o'er the rising knolls;
The white-washed church betokens rustic pride;
The river's glassy face star-mirrored rolls;
From yonder tower the mournful music tolls:
I hear the funeral notes across the water,
Chiming the requiem of gallant souls
Who died in mis'ry, 'mid the day's slaughter,
Without the soothing aid of sister, wife, or daughter.

LXXV.

'Twas a fair sight when through the village street,
With rolling drums, and banners floating gay,
And all the equipage of war complete,
The soldiers marched right gallantly away.
Then the wrinkled matron and the sire grey
Bestowed their blessing on their parting son,
And then at night retired for him to pray.
Yes! 'twas a glorious sight; but soon 'twas done,
And as the pageant passed, their sorrows had begun.

LXXVI.

Ah! there is weeping in that vale to-night,
And bosoms ready with their woes to burst.
Alas! fair maiden, with thine eye once bright,
No more within thy breast may love be nursed;
Of dark despair thy heart now feels the worst;—
Thy soldier lover sleeps the sleep of death!
Well mayst thou say of wars, "Be all accurs'd!"
"Perchance he called me with his gasping breath?
I come, my love! I come.—But, ha! Can this be Death!"

LXXVII.

"He died in honor, sir! I saw him fall."
"Ha! you saw him, then! Oh, where?" "At the head
Of his brave comrades. At his captain's call
He scaled the heights, and there in honor bled."
"Twas Honor, then? but, ah! you say he's dead!
Thus mad with grief, the grey-haired sire spake.—
"Keep your honor—give me my boy instead!"
"But, hold! he battled for his country's sake."
"My God! must men in blood their savage fury slake?"

LXXVIII.

"Honor? Give me my boy! Away with fame,
 If it is built upon eternal wo.
 Give me his life; I'll ask nor noble name,
 Nor gaudy wreaths that fickle men bestow!
 Makes Fame our happiness on earth? Ah, no:
 The glory take, and give his being back!—
 My own brave boy! and must thy spirit go
 Before its time along yon devious track?
But that's to Heaven, while I must writhe upon the rack."

LXXIX.

Oh! ye who madly pant for martial fame,
 With calm reflection for a moment pause,
 And calculate the price of such a name.
 Say what it is, will be, and what it was;—
 Trampling on God's, if not on earthly laws;
 And every laurel makes a widow's tear!
 It does not matter what may be the cause,
 Thy glories still are purchased deadly dear,
And all must rise like ghosts from some poor soldier's bier.

LXXX.

Let's leave the world, and 'neath some spreading tree
Commune with Nature. 'Tis the noblest aim
Of man to let his reason wander free
O'er Nature's works. The world, with all its fame,
Yields nothing but the hist'ry of our shame,
Our crimes, our vanities; and more than these,
The magic ringing of a worshipped name!
Some parasite that rose the mob to please,
And like a feather floats upon its fickle breeze.

LXXXI.

Come, sweet Sylvania! with thee let me rove
(Thy own soft smiles to lure me farther on)
Through all the windings of the verdant grove;
Beneath the archway of each hanging stone,
With lichen weed, and creeping moss o'ergrown;
Whose time-worn surface, 'neath the light of day,
Unfolds the mystic tale of times bygone;—
Not to the soulless of this mortal clay,
But that which lives in dreams beneath poetic sway.

LXXXII.

A moment here, beside this tree we'll rest,—
Our downy couch the brown-tinged moss shall be.
Here, may we feel how sweet on Nature's breast
It is to sink and slumber pleasantly;
Lulled by the song of birds, whose melody
Might be angelic, if we did but dream,
And dreaming, mingle in the revelry
Of Fancy's sportive sprites, whose sunny gleam,
Reflecting in the spell, with airy shades would teem!

LXXXIII.

To lull the senses to a sweeter sleep
From yon low vale the flow'rets' perfumes rise,
And from the hardy shrubs along the steep;—
Borne by the softest airs of Summer's skies,
The fragrant rose, and from the deeper dyes
Of the meek violet, a breath ascends
That thrills the nostrils with a rich surprise.
The blushing flower, as it opening bends,
Unfolds its juicy cell, whose sweetness Nature lends.

LXXXIV.

Who cannot see in each unfolding flower
The glorious Maker's palpable impress?
The wide-spread hand of Heaven's almighty power
Delights e'en the tiny flower to caress!
The slightest shrub of earth doth claim no less
The kindly aid of Nature's nurt'ring law
Than the lofty oak, whose boughs seem to press
The low-arched canopy, whence angels saw
Old Night roll back her clouds with deep, mysterious awe.

LXXXV.

This is the poet's home. Here Nature wild
Doth breathe enchantment's airs on all around.
It seems as if some angel spirit smiled
On this green roof, and swept this mossy ground,
And left it blest. The breeze with whistling sound
Trips o'er th' umbrageous boughs; enthrals the ear—
Not as through the Egyptian towers wound
Æolian sweets; but more constant; clear
As angel's voice, if such our souls may sometimes hear!

LXXXVI.

Monarch of the woods! Centuries have rolled
Their circling orbits 'round thy aged head!
The yellow tinges of autumnal gold
Have changed thy green, as years their seasons led.
This is thy summer robe; the Winter fled
On the merry wind, chased by buoyant Spring:
The hail and snow, that so lately hurtled
O'er thee, have ceased their symphonies to ring,
And countless dancing leaves around thy branches cling.

LXXXVII.

Giant oak! Type of the unbending mind!
Thou standest there in kingly solitude,—
Unscathed by passing years of wintry wind,
That whistled loud in boist'rous music rude,—
Of Nature's stamp with nobleness imbued,
The adoration of the forest scene!
Amidst changes around thee thou hast stood
In naught varying but thy youthful mien,
And that as age creeps on assumes a deeper green.

LXXXVIII.

Canst from thy womb unfold a tale of yore—
Breathe it in music from thy rattling crest—
Ere bold COLUMBUS trod this unknown shore?
Did savage hordes beneath thy roofing rest,
Ere warfare's weapons pierced each hating breast?
Did the tremendous mammoth's mountain tread
(That monster beast, the wonder of the west!)
Pass thee by and shake thy towering head?
What bones repose beneath—what bosoms here have bled?

LXXXIX.

Alas! what is man! E'en if passing time
Should write a tale on Nature's queenly face,
(And such there are in mysteries sublime,)
He could not comprehend a single trace:
Although her fairest works he may deface,
And claim to understand her every law,
Yet she moves on with proud, majestic pace,
And wins perchance from him a moment's awe,
And what with her is right to him appears a flaw.

XC.

To me at times all forms are beautiful;
The earth, the sky, and every living thing.
And when from garden or hill-side I cull
A bunch of flowers, their perfume seems to bring
Beauty from the earth on its airy wing;
For thence it drew its sweets. That rich, dark loam,
Helped by the nurt'ring smile of ruddy Spring,
Gave all that flower owns—its beauty's home;—
And thus to me all things are fair 'neath Heaven's dome.

XCI.

The many-colored earth—the full-arched sky—
The invisible air that rides between—
Affordeth food to Contemplation's eye.
—All is beautiful—the seen and th' unseen.
The fields and forests liveried in green;
A clear brook babbling in the Summer's sun;
A mountain towering with majestic mien;
Give a picture, suggesting, one by one,
Unnumbered thoughts the soul has not the power to shun.

XCII.

Our visual sense is colored by the mind,
And if distemper broods upon the brain
Naught of healthy hue can the victim find.
And so with diff'rent men. The rustic swain
Plods o'er green fields, and deems his task a pain;
While the poet looks with a lover's eye,
That never seems to tire, but looks again;
And in the fields and woods that 'round him lie
He sees new things to love, and scarcely knoweth why.

XCIII.

What is it that makes us love? A plain face
May please as well as one that's young and fair;
And we may call it beautiful, and trace
Some trait that we may think beyond compare,
While others at our lack of taste may stare.
Their thoughts are not then ours, for they reveal
Nothing that beauteous forms we think should wear.
What throbs are those which through our senses steal
At Beauty's view? 'Tis that which makes us *think* and *feel!*

XCIV.

The lordly savage roved this wilderness,
Along yon valley chased the flying deer;
And Indian maidens bathed their loveliness
In this meand'ring crystal stream; and here
The watchful sentry saw the foe appear;—
Not with the martial sound of kettle-drum,
But panthered step, that scarcely meets the ear,
And mingled with the low, half-uttered hum [come!"
Of deadly hate; and now, the wild war-whoop—" We

XCV.

But he has gone; nor left a trace behind,
Save where the spade reveals his sires' dust
To stranger's gaze. Perchance it is designed
That we, proud minions of Ambition's lust,
From this, our stage, by stronger arms be thrust,
And o'er our ashes other nations tread.
Weep for thy race, poor man! for fade it must.
Forget not with thy fate is Nature wed,
And Nature's every change is numbered by her dead.

XCVI.

In classic Greece the Muse first tuned her lute,
And at the touch the graces breathed complete,
And Music's self seemed roused, no longer mute.
Soon from the trembling chords vibration sweet
Tripped its light cadence on poetic feet:
The first of poets seized th' immortal lyre—
(Then Fame looked smiling down from her high seat,)
Invoked Olympus' gods the theme t' inspire,
While sweetest symphony danced o'er the golden wire!

XCVII.

And as he breathed with noblest passion wrought,
Music's spirits bestowed their sweetest tongue,
And Nature bursted from the heaving thought.
Of Trojan and of Grecian arms he sung,
And states in rapture o'er the music hung.
A victor thus, her skill again she tried;
A gaudy banner to the breeze she flung;—
To crown her hopes arose the Drama's pride;
And thus she grew to fame, with Nature for her guide.

XCVIII.

The school of art—the school of morals too;
(Not such as now that Drama has become,
Where everything is shown but what is true:)
And here she flourished 'neath the Thespian dome,
Where all the graces found a welcome home,
Until the brightest days of Greece were o'er,
When e'en paled the glory of mighty Rome,
And then she sank, as if to rise no more;
But soon she sprang to life upon a happier shore.

XCIX.

Alas! for Science when the savage horde,
Led roaring on by Havoc's scathing sway,
Rushed from the North, while swift Destruction's sword
Cleaved unrelentingly its dreadful way,
And turned to blackest night Art's dawning day!
The Muse in sadness brooded o'er the scene,
Where all her noble works dismantled lay,
And mourned her fading laurels once so green—
Wept o'er her present woes, and what she might have been.

C.

At length the Arts revived; the crusade came;
Kings poured their arms to holy Palestine;
And minstrelsy lit up th' expiring flame
That once had glowed on Poesy's sainted shrine,
When man had worshipped her as half divine.
She reached no lofty song;—the troubadour,
To praise a lady, or to wreathe the wine,
Strewed her pearls alone from shore to shore;—
His songs were tuned to love, and blent with mythic lore.

CI.

Though PETRARCH sang the warmest lays of love,
And wild BOCCACCIO told the pleasant tale,
And DANTE's own fire seemed ta'en from heavenly Jove;
Though Spanish ballads turned to deadly pale
The peasant's cheek: yet each of these must fail,
And e'en the master touches of MOLIERE,
To equal him; and all can but avail
To give a shadow of our own SHAKSPEARE—
The man the Nine adore—the man we all revere.

CII.

Nature's fav'rite! how we sink before thee!
All poetry by thine is nothingness.—
Immortal bard! can such another be,
Or must the art divine grow less and less?
The secrets of the fates we cannot guess;
But this we know, from what has been, that earth
Has had her poet, garbed in Nature's dress.
The lapse of years could give but one such birth,
Nor countless ages match SHAKSPEARE's matchless worth.

CIII.

Besides the master there are lesser lights
That blaze above mankind like brilliant stars,—
Elected priests of Poesy's sweet rites,
Whose laurels ne'er were won in bloody wars,
But from the symphony of tripping bars.
MILTON, whose lyre was Heaven's own sublime;
And faultless POPE, who ne'er a couplet mars;
Great DRYDEN, of the full, resounding rhyme;
And lastly, though not least, the CHILDE of later time.

CIV.

But, ah! there should not pass unmentioned here,
Those of the softer lute, the sweeter lay.
For KEATS and COLLINS shed the pitying tear,
And weave the laurel wreath for classic GRAY;—
SHELLEY, whose life was but a dreamer's day:
And drink the lethean draughts of SPENSER's "Queen."
A moment linger with the linnet GAY;
With simple CRABBE feast on the rustic scene; [been.
Pause by WORDSWORTH's tomb—and think what he has

CV.

Bard of the North! A world has heard thy lyre!—
Immortal BURNS! Oh, weak the poet's art
To tell thy worth. We can but gaze; admire
Thy meteor flight; weep for thy noble heart
Crushed by the rude world, that feels not the smart
Of spirit pain; the stinging, racking wo
To feeling souls its coldness doth impart;
To thee what matters all we now bestow—
Canst hear thy paens sung when thou art slumbering low?

CVI.

Poet of the heart! Nature's wayward child!
Thou of the sadly sympathetic shell!
Who has not mourned the lovely vale defiled,
The village that thy pencil drew so well?
We almost hear the melancholy knell
That tolled sweet Auburn's loss; or feel the pain
Of the musing Traveller's sad farewell;
And hope the world may see thy like again.
Alas! the Nine doth sigh, such prayers are poured in vain!

CVII.

Hail! wildest passion of the human breast!
Bauble of the mad, idol of the wise—
Alike by peasant and by prince possessed—
Sweet, all-pervading Love. The lover sighs
And draws mute rapture from his mistress' eyes!
The solace of our prime, whose constant bliss
All the famed riches of the East out-vies.
Man braves the world—commits a crime—for this,
That he may live an hour on woman's honeyed kiss!

CVIII.

Sweet woman's arts, and gentle woman's wiles,
Through the long ages of our mortal span,
Have swayed, and ever will with winsome smiles
The heart, the mind, the every deed of man;
All worship her; resist her smiles who can?
The man of honor, and the truckling knave,
Pant 'neath the flutter of her magic fan;
Each to her wild whim is a servile slave;
And e'en for woman sighs the hermit in his cave!

CIX.

A lovely maiden is the budding rose,
Whose op'ning beauty, like its blushing own,
Soft fragrance o'er the human garden throws;
And woman is the gentle flower blown,
Where man is taught to build his earthly throne.
His queen—his goddess; nor may fairer be.
Could man, deprived of woman, left alone
On this wide earth, the least of pleasure see,
Or bear th' incubean weight of dull mortality?

CX.

On her, the victim of mistaken love
Pale Melancholy shows her leaden eye,
While every joy doth cank'ring Wo reprove;
The weary hours like ages gliding by,
Until the longing spirit fain would die.
For life's a desert waste, and all that was
Can never be again; Love's fountain's dry,
And parched with dearth of hope; and it must pass
To deep forgetfulness, while woman cries, Alas!

CXI.

And must we part—and have we loved in vain?
Ah! me, 'twere better we had never met!
And shall I never hear that voice again,
And has our sun of love in darkness set?
Those eyes have looked their last with weeping wet!
And shall I press those melting lips no more?
'Tis true—'tis true! But can I e'er forget?
Night looms apace; the morn of life is o'er;
My barque is launched; adieu to thee and Boyhood's shore.

CXII.

Forget thee? As fixed as the sun on high,
As man to earth, is mem'ry bound to thee!
The stars shall cease their duty in the sky,
Ere thou from constant thought shalt banished be!
And when I'm tossed alone on Life's wild sea,
A homeless, hapless man, my mind will turn
To pictured scenes of bliss with love and thee;
Ah! then how sadly will my bosom burn
To have thee shed a tear upon my friendless urn!

CXIII.

Clime of the West! young Freedom's rugged home
Was rudely reared upon thy savage breast.
The wind's wild music and the billows' foam
Startled thine eagle from his rocky nest
Upon thy sea-girt coast, as if possessed
Of ardor such as those who freely gave
Their starried ensign, emblem of the West,
In Heaven's ethereal airs to brightly wave,
And freedom win beneath, or welcome Honor's grave!

CXIV.

Spirits of that stormy time! Glory's wreathes
Were never twined for nobler brows than yours!
Above your tombs the soul of Freedom breathes
Immortal fame; and e'en on other shores,
Where thy genius, Liberty, seldom soars,
Where regal masters rule—a tyrant horde—
The fettered slave his prayer in secret pours
For Heaven to grant such men to draw his sword,
And proud defiance hurl against his feudal lord.

CXV.

Herculean labors stared ye in the face;
But these increased the nerve to stem the strife
For liberty and justice. Lived one so base
To bargain honor for that poor thing, life?
Who would not gladly greet the warring knife,
If dying thus he could bequeath a name
To time unsullied, alone with virtue rife?
Alas! there have been such; their country's shame!
But they can never live in Virtue's cherished fame.

CXVI.

Blessed by approving Heaven the altar rose,
And Glory came her choicest wreathes to twine:
Then like receding waves rolled back her foes.
Devoted hearts attended near the shrine,
Libations made, and poured the ruby wine,
While Freedom's stars came twinkling one by one,
And settled 'round that spirit, half divine;
Then her flag beamed and glittered in the sun,
As millions blessed the worth—the deeds of WASHINGTON.

CXVII.

Great man! Thy life hath left to hist'ry's page
The purest record of thy country's fame!
In vain we praise the heroes of an age;
Like the autumnal leaves, before thy name
They crumble into dust; they cannot claim
One laureled leaf, which 'round thy noble brow
The Past hath girt;—the Future still the same:
Revolving years will to thy deeds bestow
Their meed of just applause, that adds a brighter glow.

CXVIII.

Columbia, weep, that Slav'ry's hated crime,
In deepest dye of foul, unnatural stain,
Should be emblazoned on thy book of time.
Freer the world has grown, and Slav'ry's chain
No more bids Murder stalk across the main,
Where gauntest Misery in frenzy glowed,
Closing the fest'ring links of mortal pain.
No more doth shrinking Commerce bear the load
Of human flesh and blood on swift Destruction's road.

CXIX.

E'en when the mighty empress of the sea,
Whose countless sails remotest ocean sweep,
Has washed from her shrine the foul iniquity,
Must she still sleep, the noblest country sleep,
While Freedom's guardian angels blushing weep?
Lives none to pluck the venom at its source?
Men we have who'd dare the Tarpean leap,
But few to feel a shadow of remorse.
And doth Columbia own no giant WILBERFORCE?

CXX.

Can custom always reign? Believe it not.
There is a better time for earth; man may
Fetter his fellow, but 'tis ne'er forgot;
And Retrospection's view brings on the day
When merit only makes superior clay.
To see the unworthy past, will man incite
To tear the flimsy gauze of sin away—
Acknowledging no thought but what is right;
And then indeed the earth looms up from Error's **night.**

CXXI.

Stern Justice banishes each paltry fear,
Obedient to the calls of her high trust;
While Mercy reasons with her softest tear.
Pause, Columbia; ask if it is just
That one should toil to please another's lust.
Dost say 'tis true? Then where does Justice **dwell,**
If she thus leaves to shame man's meaner dust?
Or has she aped some common fiend of hell,
And to her former self has sighed a last farewell!

CXXII.

But " we are free !" so would our poets sing;
And thundered such by each aspiring sage.—
" Free as the soarings of our eagle's wing."
—Free as the lion in his iron cage;—
Nay, as the puppet on his wired stage!
Just were our sires: an expedient rule,
Blessed by the tut'rings of a backward age,
Has taught us justice in another school;
Of each ambitious knave we're made the sportive tool!

CXXIII.

Oh, may not penitential years erase
The spots that soil our fame; for soiled it is:
When Slav'ry dare not show its gorgon face!
But Order startles.—Anarchy is this,
When man enjoys his manumission's bliss?
Old th' institution is. Unhappy time,
When man will not his craven fears dismiss;
But still must cringe and tolerate a crime.
—Say, must we fall in sin, and ne'er to virtue climb?

CXXIV.

By heaven! it makes me blush for man, to see
Some whining sniv'ler pand'ring body, soul,
And all that makes him God's image, that he
May bask in public favor: while the whole
Inertia of his acts tends to control
And bury conscience! Is he a man, whose noon,
Whose prime of life, nor heeds that inward toll,
That strikes the noble mind, but who will soon
Kneel at the foot of power, and crave a beggar's boon ?

CXXV.

Then let me be a dog, and lick the hand
That feeds me; for of all I do detest
The sycophant, that serpent of the land.
To be a dog, is to be among the best
Of brutes; but he's of mankind the meanest:
A paltry villain and a truckling knave.
And doth Columbia cherish at her breast
Such scorpions; and doth her banner wave
Alike o'er shameless deeds and o'er the PATRIOT's grave !

CXXVI.

Thou shalt not lie; but Truth's Damascean blade
Should not be wielded in too bold a sun,
Lest too much light may make mankind afraid.
'Tis not by force the battle's always won;
Yet he who loves the world will never shun
The task of scanning well the passing time;
To cure distemper ere the root's begun;
Nor shrink to show the nakedness of crime,
In all its sickly stench, its foul and loathsome slime.

CXXVII.

FRANCE sleeps and wakes both at the self-same time—
Still clings to the poor relics of her lord.
Oh, may she rise, repenting of her crime;—
Not as of yore, when blood like water poured,
And Freedom gasped beneath th' avenging sword,—
When madly, like the mountain torrent's flow,
Rushed to the scene Progression's victimed horde.
The hand that felled Oppression dealt the blow
That laid the guiltless form of Freedom's goddess low.

CXXVIII.

Oh! retribution deep—unhappy land!
When he, the spoiler, providential came:
Thy brightest glories glitt'ring in his hand.
But all that glory gave was martial fame,
The meanest morsel of a people's shame.
Ambition's lover led thy crusade's van;
Conquest appeared to be his cherished aim.—
Crime followed guilt, and blood more plenteous ran,
When France, forgetting Heaven, bowed and worshipped
[man!

CXXIX.

Peace to the Past! The Future be thy hope.
'Tis ne'er too late from Error to recede.
Too deeply has thou revelled. The fell scope
Of passion unrestrained, has made thee bleed
What ages cannot cleanse. Thy present need
A man of merit—and of morals too.
Not one who swayeth like the toppling reed;
But, like th' unbending oak, be constant, true,
And capable to see with wide expansive view.

CXXX.

What if thy children's tears in rivers run,
Will fading hope now sink, nor rise again
To be the herald of thy future sun?
His bones may whiten earth; but not in vain
The death of him in Freedom's battles slain.
His wasted ashes lie on Honor's bier,
'Neath the proud canopy of Glory's fane:
Unnumbered hearts the patriot's deeds revere,
And to his memory drop Affection's welcome tear!

CXXXI.

His name's a legacy, that Hist'ry's page,
(Not with the weight of fulsome praises bowed,)
Bequeaths, exulting, to a future age!
His grave's the world—eternity his shroud;
Blessed by the lowly, worshipped by the proud;
The bane of kings—whose monument's their shame;
His station fixed above the common crowd;
No tongue can taint—no scathing years defame—
The amaranthine wreaths that cluster 'round his name!

CXXXII.

But I must push my song; for much of sin
And wo, and misery, doth yet remain.
—Is't strange that vice and wealth should be akin;
That poverty inflicts no deeper stain
Than the rank desire for ill-gotten gain?
'Tis custom stamped, although 'tis not innate,
To have no feeling for your fellow's pain.
'Tis no less with rich or poor.   All separate
Their interests from the crowd—indifferent to its fate.

CXXXIII.

The courtezan parades the public street,
On poor and ragged virtue smiles in scorn.
Yes! smile, thou pampered thing! the Present's sweet;
But turn one searching glance to young Life's morn.
What seest thou?   Nay, start not.   'Tis to be borne.
"I see a bright-eyed girl, not yet thirteen,
Whose bud of happiness contains no thorn;
The sire and matron sit upon the green;
The lowing herds at eve complete the rustic scene."

CXXXIV.

Five years have passed. The moon is up, and bright
Her rays are dancing o'er the moss-girt stream.
For love and lovers 'tis a splendid night!
I see a maiden and a youth. The dream
Of love is full upon them :—by the beam
Of the pale moon he views her matchless charms,
And swears he loves. Are oaths what oft they seem?
At first meek Virtue whispers faint alarms—
Nay, nay! she cries, then sinks into his circling arms.

CXXXV.

Betrayed and ruined: here thou might'st have paused,
And started back affrighted from the deed.
'Tis not by adding crime that guilt is glossed;
'Tis made the loathsomer. Our passions feed
On strong desire, and quickly take the lead
Of every act.—Alas! when black Despair
Beheld thy tortured bosom vainly bleed,
Thy fate was sealed; so innocent, so fair.
To sink a spotted thing in Sin's enslaving snare!

CXXXVI.

Dost like the picture? Nay, I have not done;
Thy heart shall ache if thou hast conscience left.
I speak of one who called thee daughter; one
Who loved thee as herself: of one who crept
To watch how sweet her fav'rite slept.
When disease racked, and fever scorched thy brow,
Who soothed thee thro' the night? Ah, canst forget?
Has the warm gush of feeling ceased to flow?
If thou dost think of her, weep for thy mother now!

CXXXVII.

For she is dead! Died of a broken heart!
She could not face a sneering world that knew
Her daughter's shame. 'Twas bitter thus to part,
Yet better than to see thee in the hue
Of youthful bloom, so guilty to the view.
But what's death to *thee?* Thou hast not within
That barren breast one throb to friendship true!
Perchance thou thinkst at times what thou hast been,
Wilt be, and what thou art, thou parasite of sin!

CXXXVIII.

Thou mayst revel now; but the time shall come
When e'en the rouge will cease to make thy cheek
Beam luringly on man. Then shall be dumb
The flatt'rers of thy prime, as pale and weak
Thou fadeth to the tomb. No one shall speak
The kindly voice of love in soothing tone.
Then wilt thou think of her, who, fond and meek,
Bent o'er thy youthful bed; but long since gone,
And thou, repenting late, in misery left alone.

CXXXIX.

Cold blew the sweeping blast of wintry wind;
The driving snow had filled December's sky;
The falling flakes a weary trav'ller blind,
Who crawls with giddy pace and tearful eye.
In trembling anguish bursts the smothered sigh
From Woman's soul. Close to her shelt'ring breast
She hugs her babe to warm it ere it die.
The fierce storm's rattle lulls it to its rest,
Nor wakes till life is o'er, then revels with the blest.

CXL.

Phrenzied by pain and want, that woman's face
Betrays the haggard aspect of despair;
But once it shone with Beauty's matchless grace.
Her first, her latest crime, that she was fair;
Was wooed and won by man, whose love, like air,
Stops but to taste the fragrance of the flower!
Thoughtless, she fell into the demon's snare,
Confiding in his word. Unhappy hour,
When LEILA and her love held trysting in her bower!

CXLI.

Oh, Faith! thou sweetest daughter of the skies!
To rule thy birth, what magic shone divine,
And made thy sanctuary in woman's eyes?
Nor fairer altar be; but, ah! they shine
From the sad frailties of a fallen line!
Her constancy shall meet with no return,
Though man may pledge her name in rosy wine,
And she her hapless fate must shortly learn,
And weep her soul away o'er young Love's broken urn!

CXLII.

She was the fairest of the village train;
Of all the fav'rite, and her parents' pride;
The source of wo to many a sighing swain.
Her humble cot, upon a green hill-side,
Lay clasped in flowers, whose twinings seemed to glide
Around, as if to shield it from the wind;
Like gay Hope, standing by the dreamer's side,
But withers with the frost. So Hope is kind
In genial hours, but flees when cares beset the mind.

CXLIII.

He saw her but to love; with flatt'ring art,
Taught by the follies of a city's maze,
He won the rustic maiden's guileless heart;
Yet for a time his dark design delays—
Feeding her ravished soul with honeyed praise:
Too artless she such garnish to contemn;
Believes his promises of future days.
Thus for a while he kissed the beauteous gem,
Then left the fading flower to wither on its stem.

CXLIV.

Wo! to her parents' love of honest fame!
Alas! for her, the lily of the vale!
Bowed down with guilt to misery and shame!
Imploring Pity fain would cease the tale
Of wretched LEILA's grief, so fair, so frail.
—She still believes; and on her fatal bed
Turns to the lake to see his well-known sail:
She cheers her parents, that he yet will wed:
For him she wildly raves, while fever racks her head.

CXLV.

But he, forgetful of his sylvan maid,
Had won a high-born lady for his bride.
True, she was fair; but she he had betrayed
Was fairer yet when blooming in her pride,
Ere all but love with maiden honor died.
But she was poor—her lot was lowly cast—
Unfitted then with wealth to be allied.
Yes! he had ruined her; but that was past;
And, though it was a sin, that deed should be the last!

CXLVI.

Away with conscience! 'tis a festive night—
A wedding feast among the rich and great.
The lamps are burning with their lustrous light,
And courteous men on beauteous women wait,
Amid the pomp of Fashion's pampered state.
Sweet music vibrates o'er the tap'stried wall,
While Wit and Pleasure keep Youth, Beauty, late.
The bride and bridegroom glide along the hall,
And with reluctance stay from Hymen's sportive call.

CXLVII.

'Tis past the noon of night. The merry dance
Ne'er flags, but flies on music-moving feet,
And softer grows fair woman's kindling glance,
While lamps may yet with rosy morn compete.
The silk-clad nymph heeds not the snowy sleet,
Nor e'en the whistling of the wintry wind;
But ragged LEILA in the frozen street
Is shiv'ring at its blast. Could she but find
The lover of her youth, oh, would he yet be kind!

CXLVIII.

She sees the lordly mansion proudly piled ;—
She stops to rest upon its steps of stone ;
And closer still she hugs her frozen child ;
Ah ! now indeed she feels herself alone—
Her pledge of love and shame forever gone !—
She kneels upon the ice,—devoutly prays,—
Asking if these, her suff'rings, may atone,
Not for hers, but his crime : no curse she lays
Upon his guilty head ; but hopes him blissful days !

CXLIX.

An opened shutter shows the lighted room—
The gorgeous revelry of wealth within—
Contrasting strangely with the outward gloom ;
Here, LEILA, shivering in rags and sin,
In sorrow ponders o'er what she has been ;
There, proud beauty moves with a scornful eye.
—One look she catches ere the rites begin ;
That quenches hope ; 'twere better now to die.
" My God, 'tis him !" she screams in wild, distracted cry !

CL.

Enough! her hopes are ashes; and her heart,
Her all of feeling, withered into dust.
Alas! too true when he had said, "We part!"
But for an hour? Forever! Yes, die she must,
Th' unhappy victim of a demon's lust!
Is death for her—is she not fair and young?
Alas! with woman's woes she has been cursed;
Nor can she e'er forget that honeyed tongue
That ruined her, and o'er whose tones she breathless hung.

CLI.

Look on that figure, man; for it is dead!
With calmness may you gaze upon it now.
How glassy beams that eye deep in her head,
And yet its fire is quenched. Upon that brow,
Where once your kisses breathed a lover's vow,
Meek resignation to her hapless fate
Sits like an angel throned. But, see! the glow
Of Hope had flickered to the last:—too late!
Too late it came, for she lies here in deathly state!

CLII.

Where is the fun'ral robe, the hearse, the pall,—
Those solemn things which tell us of the tomb?
Has crape concealed the gilding of your wall?
Do noiseless feet betray the gen'ral gloom?
Doth Sorrow sit in weeds in every room?
No : 'tis a phantasy. Away ! away !
The bride appears in Beauty's blushing bloom.
—Bury this beggar ! Who would not be gay,
And quaff the cup of joy upon his wedding day !

CLIII.

Yes ! let him hear it ; and when years have flown,
That piercing cry shall ring upon his ear,
Turning his recreant heart to moveless stone,
Shaking his palsied form with guilty fear.
And then may some sad spirit, hov'ring near,
Give the faint outline of his LEILA's form ;
Her glassy eye bedimmed by one hot tear ;
But naught remaining of her maiden charm ;
And then a passing gust proclaim that wintry storm

CLIV.

Yes! let him hear it, when his blameless bride
Dandles his baby offspring on her knee,
And he smiles on the scene with father's pride,
Stooping to kiss the lips of infancy,
Wrapped in dreams of his boy's futurity.
But, hark! whence comes that cry so deathly wild,
Like some despairing wretch in agony;
But sinking now, as angel's whispers mild,
It strikes upon his ear, " Where, where is LEILA's child?"

CLV.

What's boasted Pride, but rank, superfluous breath,
The surfeits of a mind diseased? How vain
While striving 'gainst th' unwelcome hand of death!
Does 't administer to the body's pain—
Or rather bid each muscle writhe again?
For man, once pampered, is a puny thing;
At every wo will whiningly complain.
When Slander foul inflicts her poisoned sting,
What aid can boasted Pride unto the mortal bring?

CLVI.

He who builds on this, is like the school-boy
Disporting bubbles on the summer air;
Awhile in safety floats the tiny toy,
Then fades away. 'Tis thus the transient glare
Of Pride looks beautiful and passing fair,
But lives upon a smile; when that has fled—
His very heart in nakedness laid bare,—
He sinks despairingly; and all is dead
Which that deluding blaze a moment brightly fed!

CLVII.

Untoward was LEILA's fate. Was thine less so,
Whose name I would not lightly mention here,
Thou who hast felt thy share of mortal wo,—
Deprived of all on earth thou heldst most dear?
Ah! few can know the deathly, blighting sear,
That scorched the aspirations of thy youth—
Left thee to shed in vain the secret tear!
Pity thou wouldst not take; but 'tis, in sooth,
A gen'rous sympathy that prompts this tale of truth.

CLVIII.

Not as a woman meets her lover, gay
In the allurement of her loveliness,
Waiting in joy, yet wond'ring at his stay;
No lover's pains were mine; no soft caress
Of those that love, which mingleth their distress—
Throwing delirium's joy around the soul:
Wrapped in the silence of my pensiveness,
I saw, but not to love; nor could control
The thought which hailed thee first from cancer to the pole.

CLIX.

A peerless woman! Such as bards have sung,
But seldom seen. Pride of the blooming West!
A Heaven of Poesy would lack the tongue
To sing but half thy worth; though 'tis impressed
Upon my every thought, rich Fancy, dressed
In the full beauty of her gayest hour,
Would need the master-touch, but half expressed
E'en when a RAPHAEL paints with magic power,
To stamp the full impress of Nature's fairest flower!

CLX.

Lady! I saw thee in my boyhood days,
Ere I had tuned my lute to love or fame;
Ere I had known that Beauty seeks its praise,
Or Virtue shrinks from vice-polluting shame!
Nor here shall adulation with thy name
Be linked. Thy name? I wear it in my heart!
Sweet retrospection is the poet's aim!
Thy praise? 'Tis honest—void of flatt'ring art,—
And of my benison is Friendship's humble part.

CLXI.

Lady! when circling years their orbits rolled,
I gazed upon thy placid brow once more;
Still thou wert lovely; but a tale was told
By the forced calmness of thine eye, which tore
My aching heart. Life's joy with thee was o'er.
Thou lovedst him not, thy plighted, bosomed lord;
Thy hopes were wrecked on young Love's rocky shore!
He loved thee not, the man thou hadst adored
Ere Fate relentingly thy sufferings deplored!

CLXII.

Thy babes may cluster at thy tender breast,
Their elfin joys may win a smile from thee—
Like crushed Love peering from its prisoned nest;
But thus a moment; thou canst never be
Again the maid who thought futurity
Was big with blissful hope. Anguish darted,
Falcon-like, upon thy fair revelry,
Rent the veil; thy love, alas! departed,—
Left thee in thy bloom, forsaken, broken-hearted!

CLXIII.

Lady, farewell! In other climes I may
Find other hearts, nor heedless of my song;
But Mem'ry, faithful on my wand'ring way,
Will keep the fairy recollection long!
When Wit and Pleasure, 'mid the giddy throng
Of Fashion, bow at Folly's empty shrine,
And when my passion does my reason wrong,
My noblest thought shall be for thee and thine—
For thee shall songs be sung, for thee shall goblets shine!

CLXIV.

How deep the throbs which thrill the wand'rer's vein,
Who, melancholy, roves a distant strand,
And hears, in some half-sung, half-chaunted strain,
The well-known music of his native land!
A spell, as if by an enchanter's wand,
Enwraps the soul; while passes to the view
Life's younger days, on which the chilling hand
Of Time has left no blast.   Their early hue
Looks yet as green and bright as Fancy ever drew!

CLXV.

There is a spell in Music's gentle tone,
Which calls the phantoms up of what has been;
But sweetest far when listening alone,
And sadly sweet when absent from the scene!
Who has not felt, as Summer's air serene
Some plaintive strain across still waters bore,
His nerves beat high, with quickened tremor keen?
'Twas such sensations thrilled the bosom's core
Of LESTOCQ, as he paced strange on a stranger's shore.

CLXVI.

It was an air some simple rustic sang,
But he had heard it on the banks of Rhine,
When the cup was quaffed, and the loud laugh rang,
'Mong the dancers 'neath the autumnal vine.
But where are they, while he is left to pine
Alone and friendless from his land exiled,
The last descendant of a humble line?
Perished in Freedom's cause; their homes defiled,
And kingly castles high above their corpses piled!

CLXVII.

What owns man here beyond a breath of air?
Was this fair earth designed for tyrant kings,
Who seize a kingdom for their princely share,
Their only joy to point Oppression's stings,
Nor heed the woes their rank injustice brings
Upon their fellow-men; nor fear possess
For God nor man, so that the glitt'ring wings
Of Glory seem their damning cause to bless,
While Fame, reluctant, yields her magic seal's impress?

CLXVIII.

Base scourgers of the world! when man shall wake
From dark Submission's sleep; when he shall see
And feel himself oppressed; when he shall shake
The shackles from his mind, and stand forth free,
Untrammeled, in his native dignity,
Claiming an equal right with all the world;
Then, ye foul oppressors! then shall there be
A gladsome shout, while Freedom's flag 's unfurled,
And king and sceptres all from thrones polluted hurled!

CLXIX.

I saw a rocky height beleaguered 'round
By Freedom's friends; their number, few at first,
Increased by scores, until the swelling sound
Of countless men with resolution burst
Like ocean's roar. To know and bear the worst
Of human ills had been their hapless lot;
But tyrants, chains, and slavery had nursed
Aspiring hopes above their servile cot;
And dreams of liberty can never be forgot.

CLXX.

Black was the feudal fortress on the steep—
The sun almost refused on it to shine.
How many chained within that prison weep,
While lords and ladies wassail with their wine!
A little luxury they might resign
To clothe the naked and the hungry feed.
Away! 't would be a humbling of their line!
They are the peers; a peasant but a weed,
For them to sweat and toil, for them to groan and bleed!

CLXXI.

Above the gloomy walls with sullen wave
A gorgeous banner dallied on the air;
But it shall be a shroud—those stones a grave—
For all that lightly laugh and revel there;
And nothing left to tell the future where
They mould'ring lie. 'Tis willed, and it shall be;
For Retribution's arm doth never spare;
Its deeds are reckoned in eternity;
Too deep its workings are for poor humanity.

CLXXII.

Hark! to the clam'rous shouts, the din of arms!
See the proud banners glitt'ring in the sun;
While the roused soldiers' fierce and loud alarms
Tell plainly that the conflict 's now begun.
Who shall first proclaim that parapet won?
With panting hopes a thousand hearts beat high.
But e'en among that gallant crowd is one
Who perils all upon a single die;
Freely he dares the worst, and yet he knows not why.

CLXXIII.

But I could tell, while pointing to the days
Of that brave patriot's youth: I could unfold
Unto his startled and astonished gaze
A strange picture.—The prison bell has tolled;
A moment—the ax falls—and dumb and cold
Lies one who battled for his country's sake:—
The winding sheet none but the widow rolled;
For Slav'ry freezes up men's hearts.—Awake!
Thou art his son, arise; to arms, and vengeance take!

CLXXIV.

A guardian spirit, brooding o'er the scene,
I saw upon a mountain near the sky;
Around her head the lightning flashes keen,
And at her feet the thunder rumbles by!
Unmoved by aught, she looks with steadfast eye
Upon the living mass of men below;
She cheers the brave with smiles; when one would fly
Night's blackness sits upon her frowning brow. [glow.
That patriot's deeds have flushed her cheek with crimsoned

CLXXV.

She stops to see his young ambition dare
The perilous step, and leave his mates behind;
Then sweeps the cloud-girt height, so wildly fair;
Her tresses floating on the wanton wind.
Her robe flies loose; no clasping girdles bind;
Hygean smiles glow on her rosy cheek;
The piercing eye proclaims the freeborn mind;
And her clear, mellow voice, nor harsh, nor weak,
Sounds like a spirit strain above the mountain's peak!

CLXXVI.

Immeasurably great, spirit of the free!
Pervading each and everything of earth—
Thy glorious essence in yon form I see—
The emblem of thy beauty and thy worth!
Who sweep'st unchained the realms that gave her birth,
The medium betwixt the world and heaven!
Unpoisoned air!—Propitious type! though dearth
May mark the march of kings, and links be driven
To bind mankind, by thee those chains shall yet be riven.

CLXXVII.

The serpent lightning leaps from rock to rock
In brilliant flashes 'round that spirit's head,
While far below those bands, in dreadful shock,
Oppose the front of war: and with the dead
Many a soldier finds a wakeless bed!
At every gasp of death that spirit weeps,
And more for brows her hand has garlanded.
—Freedom cannot move like yon lightning's leaps:
The growth is slow, but sure the harvest that she reaps.

CLXXVIII.

So long, it seemed as if whole ages there
Those hosts embattled for the breath of life;
And all the while that form in nether air
Cheered her flagging bands to renew the strife,
Nor fear the horrors of th' opposing knife;
For all must struggle who would dare be free;
And the cause is, though just, with danger rife.
—A thunder-bolt dispelled my phantasy;
I woke to find on earth still chains and slavery.

CLXXIX.

Oh, GERMANY! thy soil hath been the scene
Of many conflicts: and thy rivers ran
With life-blood, crimsoning their dark, pure green,
As kings fought for the slavery of man,
Numbering their victories by the span
Of murdered, that built their bridge to glory!
Yet, once more may some KOSSUTH lead thy van
Of panting youths and patriots hoary—
Crush the serpent's head, and leave a name to story.

CLXXX.

Willing to bear the yoke of laws that be,
If but tempered with Wisdom's kindly hand,
They hope for better days, yet bend the knee
Unto the feudal lord of all the land;
Yielding obedience to each demand;
But, like that basil that is sweet to smell
Untouched, yet bitter if 'tis crushed, they stand
Ready to serve their king, and serve him well,
Still, if a tyrant proves, each voice shall sound his knell.

CLXXXI.

Whatever clime may boast itself as free;
Whatever soul can love the noble deed;
Whenever minstrels wreath their poesy;
Wherever slaves are praying to be freed;
Wherever Freedom casts her fruitful seed;
On land, or barques that brave the stormy sea;
Man's, woman's heart, will o'er thy mis'ries bleed,
And oft through coming years the pledge shall be,
In cot or festive hall—"Kossuth and Hungary!"

CLXXXII.

Come to th' hills with me, and watch the sunlight
Bespangling jewels o'er the western sky :—
See, the rich shadows, gloriously bright,
Mingling their lucid tints with crimson dye!
To rival each their beauties seem to vie
In clearest azure and in deepest red ;
While Heaven looks like a banner spread on high,
Where fairy bands their glittering march have led,
To gild the gorgeous way that sweeps to Phœbus' bed.

CLXXXIII.

The sun has set; the vesper glow of eve
Has cast a gloaming stillness all around.
At such a time a feeling soul might grieve
O'er mortality, to this dull earth bound ;
Whose warmest hopes are buried in its ground,
Alike the mausoleum of all—the grave !
The vaunted hero sinks with trumping sound—
In cold neglect, the beautiful and brave !
Yet, there they equal lie, in dust which Nature gave.

CLXXXIV.

How like the passing day are hopes of youth!
Its morn is but a dream 'mid golden flowers,
Where everything assumes the garb of truth,
And the soul revels in Elysian bowers.
More glorious yet the glow of noontide hours;
And e'en th' approach of eve a holiday
Is lightly reckoned; but when dark night lowers,
Her hues, herald-like, magnificently gay,
Delight the ravished soul, while ebbs the life away!

CLXXXV.

From earliest youth I've loved the twilight's hour,
And sought some quiet spot to see it come.
Falling dews, as they kiss the closing flower,
And vesper as it stills the insect's hum,
These of my soul's deep joy have formed the sum
At eventide. And when the shadows press
Upon the earth from the silv'ry moon, dumb
With transport have I gazed, nor could I guess
If angel's step was there; yet loved it not the less.

CLXXXVI.

Pale Cynthia fills at length her wonted horn;
The stars burn 'round her in a circling train,
And, like a jeweled robe, her sides adorn,
Richly glittering o'er the heavenly main,—
Forming the mirror for some sighing swain,
Who knows his mistress sees their fav'rite star;
And this sweet thought recalls their mutual pain,
When he in sorrow left, to toil afar
For fortune and for fame to break Love's baleful bar.

CLXXXVII.

At such a time—at such a dreamy hour—
When sable night usurped the reign of day,
The lover lingered in his lady's bower;
One star they chose, that he, when far away,
Might think of Love beneath its placid ray;
And she to view at times the jeweled sky,
(If Truth would still retain its wonted sway,)
And bless their stella with impassioned sigh—
Breathing a prayer for him while swelled her tearful eye.

CLXXXVIII.

The stars are twinkling in their countless spheres!
I feel exalted in a night like this
Beyond the number of Conception's years!
To let wild Fancy ramble there,—it is
To me far more than other earthly bliss,
To know that Thought at least 's not chained to clay,
But may taste, perchance, some fair seraph's kiss,
And freely wander in yon bright array,
With suns and stars to pave the monarch's lightning way.

CLXXXIX.

Thou star of eve! Thou bright, thou beauteous star!
Thou beamest in yon silvery spangled net
The dim reflection of a world afar;
One gem among a thousand brighter yet,
In Night's coronial by the Master set!
Man's wonder; nor by him to be defiled;
Where nothing of earth but thought may ever get!
A world 's a spec in yon chaotic wild,
Where spheres on spheres are in perfection's order piled!

CXC.

Here may the student trace the Maker's hand,
If o'er this heavenly work his fancies brood,
And watch the movement of the magic wand.
Here may the Christian find that sav'ry food
Which suits the solace of a better mood.
Here Reason pauses in its frigid course,
A moment seems to revel with the good,
And seeks conviction at the fountain source,—
Assumes the garb of Truth, nor trembles at its force.

CXCI.

The stars that gem yon vast cerulean dome
Shine sentinels o'er those who hope and pray;
And e'en like lamps around our future home
Burn luringly, as if each twinkling ray
But shines the prelude of a brighter day!
And lambent beams unwearied vigils keep,
Till swift Aurora sweeps the Eastern way,
While Earth reposes, and her children sleep,
And in their dreams forget that they were born to weep.

CXCII.

A cloud, perchance, obscures the brilliant light
That sheds illumination o'er the skies,
And darkness broods upon the brow of Night:
So is our youth; like stars its longings rise,
And golden hopes allure the dreamer's eyes—
Like the fair mirage of an Afric clime,
That fills the weary trav'ller with surprise;
But Manhood hurries on the wings of Time,
And Age soon teaches us with its deep lore sublime.

CXCIII.

Astrclogy, 'tis said, in yonder stars
The coming fate of mortals clearly saw.
Is 't true that man may break these earthly bars,
And, with aspiring deed and partial awe,
Unfold the tenor of the Future's law?
Roll back the cloud that hides that dreamy land
Of longing hopes, and in embryo raw
Display the workings of its myst'ries grand,
And fix it to our gaze with touch of conjuror's wand!

CXCIV.

'Tis vain to cherish such a futile hope!
What here but Thought can range yon arch of blue?
That sphere's beyond the wisest mortal's scope :—
But he who would survey with searching view,
Obtains some wisdom from the heavens too;
And thus his mind a future fate may read,
If aspirations be but choice and few,—
The love of virtue is the noblest creed,
And of the tree of joy it is the only seed.

CXCV.

My Astrea! Dost mind that pictured dream
We fondly drew when wandering alone
Amid silent shades, when the latest gleam
Of day had sunk; the stars came one by one,
And Night's stillness had solemnly begun;
When hoped our throbbing hearts no years could mar
The rosy wreath which I for thee had won,
And Fancy saw thee in a sainted car,
To be my beacon light, thyself, thy name, a star?

CXCVI.

Alas! our hopes will wither in their bloom,
And what is bright and beautiful to-day,
On the morrow lies pulseless in its tomb!
On wings like the swift wind joy speeds away—
Such is the suff'ring of our mortal clay!
Like the mariner, tossed upon the sea,
We struggling strive to reach the nearest bay,
E'en though our breath be flitting gaspingly,—
Again the wave to trust, though hope forever flee!

CXCVII.

My ASTREA! when this shall meet thine eye,
I know thy thoughts with fondness wilt return
To Love's sweet hours, when raptured passion's sigh
Swelled up from hearts that mutually did burn;
And then, in deep sadness, for this frail urn
A cypress wreath, blent with the rose, thou'lt twine,
And sprinkle 't with thy tears. Here mayst thou learn
That, though my soul is bowed to Poesy's shrine,
All this wide world were naught to one sweet smile of thine!

CXCVIII.

Thus far the minstrel's unpresuming lay
In uncouth strains has held its quiet course;
Unmoved, unchecked, by what the world will say;—
Like some meand'ring rivulet, whose source
From a small spring, increases in its force;
Now gently winds beside the greenwood hills;
Now dashes o'er the rocks with roarings hoarse;
Until its mass the widening valley fills;
And thus the river grows; its life an hundred rills.

CXCIX.

And I through many scenes have vainly strayed—
'Mid sylvan nooks, along the ocean's shore;
And thus my song has idly been delayed;
But this has passed; and I shall dream no more
Of visionary things, or useless lore:
To aid my fellow-men; to speak of wrong;
To pray that Error's night may soon be o'er;
The weak assert their rights beside the strong;
For Justice, Virtue, Truth, shall be my future song.

CC.

Let others cringe and fawn upon the world,
Such thoughts have never been nor shall be mine.
Let come what will, my banner is unfurled,
And clearly on its folds my cause shall shine,
Whether its fortunes rise or erst decline.
I'd sooner live a pauper, beg my bread,
Than aught of independence to resign;
The cold, damp ground to be my only bed,
Than to surrender thought, a millionaire instead.

CCI.

How oft it haps that unknown merit dies
In the bright picture of its fairest bloom!
At length a Future bids its shades arise;
Then Justice trims her scales. Unenvied doom
When fame is meted on th' unheeding tomb!
Honor was his idol; nor would he deign
To crave Earth's smiles; preferred its deepest gloom.
But he who thus would live, nor dies in vain,
For unborn ages may reap profit from his pain!

CCII.

Speak as you think. None fear to tell their mind
But slaves, who cringe and fawn for gold, nor dare
To claim the rights of man; but, like the blind,
Ask help and aid all times and everywhere.
Than such 'tis best to be e'en like the air
That's marked by change, so that your course may be
Your own; your thoughts, your will, your acts, none share.
Such men earth may have seen, and earth may see,
By proud and free hearts known, and e'en their words as
[free.

CCIII.

Stern as the oak, yet supple as the reed,
The man that's truly good and truly great;
Who spurns with scorn a mercenary deed;
Who can undaunted bear the frowns of fate;
Who can reject the gold-bribed power of state;
Turning all acts unto a noble end;
Nor cares if plaudits may not come but late;
Of all that need the ever willing friend;
In whom Love, Charity, with Pride and Honor blend.

CCIV.

Ye who lived for the world, and not for self;
Who bore of fellow's pain a kindred part,
Nor sought, by pandering, to gather pelf;
Ye of the gen'rous, noble, feeling heart,
As Nature formed, untinged by guile or art;
Who ever turned to Want a pitying eye;—
May such graces ne'er from our line depart:
Still may we have some men, as years roll by,
To live like spotless PENN, or like a HOWARD die.

CCV.

Fame, Glory, what are they? How vain the strife
Of those who would attain the paltry prize,
And clutch it e'en with the last breath of life!
The voiceless infant to the upper skies,
Clad in the purity of Nature, flies:
Its lot is blessed beyond maturer age;
Its laurel wreath is growing while it dies;
It has no steep to climb, no war to wage,
Nor bears a loathsome part on Earth's hard-hearted stage.

CCVI.

But ere we part, oh, let me breathe a prayer
For that I love so well, my native land!
Stretching from the North to savannas fair;—
Clime of the snow-clad hills and zephyrs bland!
Oh! may no craven's sacrilegious hand
Be laid upon this altar of the West!
But bind our Union close with firmer band;
Renew the patriot's fire in every breast,
Till all the world may hail our country first and best.

CCVII.

May party broils and factious discontent
Ne'er reach the height where vandal spirits rise
O'er Right to hiss sedition, and to vent
Their self-made wrongs in treasonable cries.
To thee, great Ruler of the earth and skies,
We pray to hold such malcontents in awe,
And heed the teachings of the good and wise,
Whose love of country can o'erlook a flaw,
And freely worship at the shrine of sovereign LAW.

CCVIII.

Kind Heaven, forgive the arrogance of man,
Who prays for liberty, yet grants it not!
But let us hope such days are on the wan;
That brighter morns may be the Future's lot.
Then shall we gladly pluck the fest'ring rot
That eats the life sap of our Union's tree;
Then shall our 'scutcheon shine without a blot!
And when our cities spread from sea to sea,
Our flag shall proudly float, the standard of the FREE!

Printed in Poland
by Amazon Fulfillment
Poland Sp. z o.o., Wrocław